Deadliest Diseases of All Time

Malaria

Olivia
Donaldson

Cavendish
Square
New York

Published in 2015 by Cavendish Square Publishing, LLC
243 5th Avenue, Suite 136, New York, NY 10016

First Edition

Website: cavendishsq.com

This publication represents the opinions and views of the author based on his or her personal experience, knowledge, and research. The information in this book serves as a general guide only. The author and publisher have used their best efforts in preparing this book and disclaim liability rising directly or indirectly from the use and application of this book.

CPSIA Compliance Information: Batch #WW15CSQ

All websites were available and accurate when this book was sent to press.

Library of Congress Cataloging-in-Publication Data

Donaldson, Olivia, author.
 Malaria / Olivia Donaldson.
  pages cm. — (Deadliest diseases of all time)
 Includes index.
 ISBN 978-1-50260-095-0 (hardcover) ISBN 978-1-50260-097-4 (ebook)
 1. Malaria—Juvenile literature. 2. Malaria—History—Juvenile literature. I. Title.

 RC156.D66 2015
 616.9'362009—dc23

                              2014031013

Editor: Kristen Susienka
Senior Copy Editor: Wendy A. Reynolds
Art Director: Jeffrey Talbot
Senior Designer: Amy Greenan
Senior Production Manager: Jennifer Ryder-Talbot
Production Editor: David McNamara
Photo Researcher: J8 Media

Printed in the United States of America

Contents

Introduction — 5

one Malaria's Early History — 9

two Malaria Goes Global — 19

three The Malaria Cycle — 33

four Understanding, Treating, and Preventing Malaria — 43

five Continuing the Fight Against Malaria — 51

Glossary — 58
For More Information — 60
For Further Reading — 62
Index — 63

Introduction

I t starts like a cold or the flu, as sufferers come down with a high fever, chills, diarrhea, and vomiting. Sometimes people feel muscle pain as well. The **symptoms** may go away for a bit, but then come back. In the worst cases, it does damage to the liver, kidneys, lungs, or even the brain. If the correct **diagnosis** and treatment is not provided, it can kill its victims. Malaria is one of the planet's deadliest diseases, and it has caused human suffering for thousands of years.

The number of malaria sufferers in recent years is staggering. In 2012, more than 200 million people came down with malaria, and more than 600,000 died from the disease. While the numbers are huge, they actually represent a positive trend, since the number of people who have died from malaria decreased 42 percent globally from 2000 to 2012. Even more important is that malaria mortality decreased 49 percent in Africa, the part of the world most affected by

Every minute, a child dies from malaria.

this deadly disease. Even with these decreases, a child dies every minute from malaria, and Africa is the region where 91 percent of the world's malaria deaths happen. The disease is also prevalent in Central and South America, and Asia.

In a time when many vicious diseases are being conquered, malaria still plagues the globe. After years of seeing increases in the number of malaria cases, the total peaked in 2003, with 232 million cases. One year later, more than 1.2 million people died from malaria. Researchers set the decade of the 2000s as the "Decade to Roll Back Malaria." Many global organizations pledged to help combat the disease, and raise awareness of how to prevent it. Research continues in methods to reduce new cases, but officials say that even today, half the world's population is at risk of getting malaria. Medical officials are still looking for an effective vaccine against the disease, although many attempts have been made. Likewise, while other treatment options exist, newer resistant strains of the **parasite** that causes the disease have emerged in the past few decades, making the researchers' work even more challenging.

As the medical community continues to search for effective vaccines and treatments, as well as the best way to reduce the population of disease-carrying mosquitoes, people all around the world look to help the countries where malaria is still a top health concern. While people are unlikely to get malaria in the United States, citizens who travel globally, particularly to

Although malaria is rare in the United States, people who travel to countries where the illness is prevalent have a higher risk of contracting malaria.

high-risk regions, can contract the disease if they don't take specific preventative measures. If people exposed to malaria do not get the proper treatment, the disease can prove fatal.

Malaria has a long and complicated history. It took centuries for scientists to discover what caused the disease. Its earliest treatment options came ironically from a land that was ravaged by the disease when foreign conquerors brought the illness with them to a previously uninfected population. Even today, scientists are proposing some innovative and downright bizarre treatment options. To understand these efforts, you must first understand what malaria is, and how you can get it.

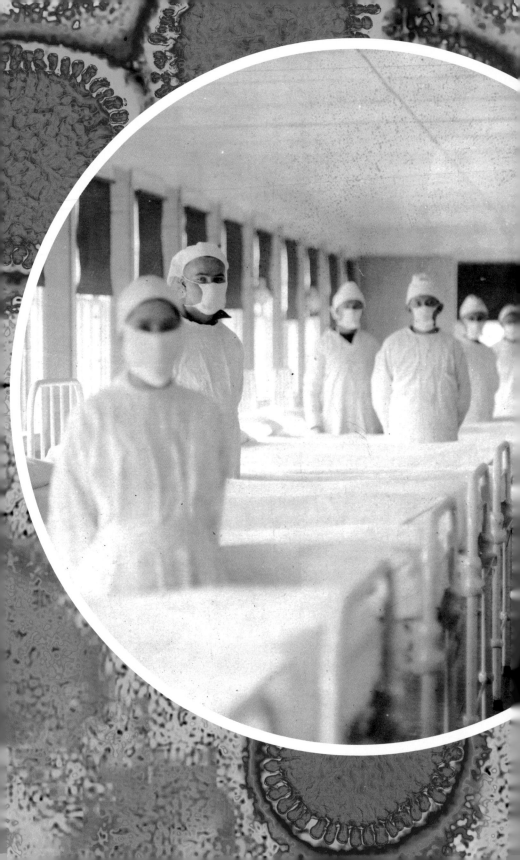

Malaria's Early History

One of the great threats to the human population is the emergence of a new or previously unidentified disease. Often, their attacks can devastate a population when people have no previous **immunity** to the illness. An early example of this type of sudden illness occurred in the early decades of the twentieth century. A strain of influenza called Spanish flu swept through the world, primarily spread by American soldiers who traveled to the European front to help neutralize the German forces. While the U.S. presence aided their allies in the battle, the influenza they brought to the continent helped create a global **pandemic**, one that would eventually claim more than 30 million victims worldwide.

The Power of Epidemics and Pandemics

An **epidemic** occurs when an infectious disease spreads beyond a local population and infects people throughout a vast region, over a long period of time.

Many deadly diseases have affected humanity, such as influenza. Here, U.S. Navy members prepare to attend to patients suffering from the illness in 1918.

European explorers arriving in the New World brought never-before-seen diseases with them. These diseases wiped out entire populations of Native people living there.

When an epidemic goes worldwide, affecting people all over the globe, it becomes a pandemic.

Before the arrival of the twentieth century, both epidemics and pandemics were leading causes of death. In fact, prior to World War I, if there was a war being waged, you were much more likely to die from an infectious disease spread by an enemy army than from the wounds inflicted by their guns and swords.

When the Spanish conquistadors came to the Americas, for instance, it wasn't their lances and swords that killed off up to 90 percent of the Native population and allowed them to colonize most of Latin America. Instead, most succumbed to the deadly diseases that the Spanish spread, including malaria, which Native Americans had never been exposed to before. The few Natives who survived were so impressed by the Christian god that seemed to protect European armies from such illnesses that they allowed themselves to be converted to Christianity. In reality, Europeans were more resistant to these deadly diseases, having lived with them for centuries.

As you can see, as a result of epidemic diseases, the entire history of the New World was completely changed. However, this is just one example of the impact epidemics can have, and have had, on this planet.

Of course, it is one thing to open up a history book and read about how, in only two years' time, close to 40 percent of Europe's population collapsed and died of being infected with a virus which caused a nasty illness called the bubonic plague. This happened in the fourteenth century, well before the discovery of much medical knowledge concerning the origin, means of transmission, treatment, prevention, and cure of many diseases. However, it is much harder to believe that at the beginning of the twenty-first century, even in the industrialized world, epidemics can have such a big impact on our lives. Just look at the havoc a disease by the name of acquired immune deficiency syndrome (AIDS) has wreaked. Not only has AIDS killed millions of people and infected even more, it has also led to major transformations in behavior and social attitudes.

Recorded History's First Disease

Of course, AIDS reared its ugly head near the end of the twentieth century. Malaria has been around since day one, or at least since people first started taking

A Closer History

6000 BCE First written reference to deadly fevers thought to be malaria.

500 BCE Greek physician Hippocrates describes cyclical nature of malaria fevers and associates the disease with swamp water.

1500s Malaria comes to America from infected European colonists and African slaves.

1630s Jesuit missionaries in Peru learn from Native people about the **antimalarial** properties of the cinchona tree. They introduce **quinine**, a powder made from the tree's bark, to Europe and Asia.

1880 First true sighting of the malaria parasite by the French doctor Alphonse Laveran.

1897 British surgeon Ronald Ross cracks the mystery of how humans are infected by malaria via mosquitoes.

1898 Italian zoologist Giovanni Batista Grassi traces the course of *plasmodium* from human to mosquito to human and identifies the Anopheles as the culprit.

1934 First synthetic version of quinine is manufactured in Germany.

1950 Launch of a global project to control malaria by spraying DDT.

1950s The World Health Organization (WHO) announces strategy for worldwide eradication of malaria.

1961 First chloroquine-resistant strains of *Plasmodium falciparum* are discovered in Thailand.

1972 Global eradication of malaria program is declared dead.

1987 Colombian biochemist Manuel Patarroyo develops the first vaccine against the *Plasmodium falciparum* parasite.

2000s "Decade to Roll Back Malaria" is declared.

2009 A new vaccine trial, developed by GlaxoSmithKline and targeting infected children, begins.

2014 As GlaxoSmithKline's vaccine trial moves farther ahead, a small rival company, Sanaria, also races to produce a more effective malaria vaccine.

notes on the strange and deadly fevers that caused entire populations to burn up and waste away (about 6000 BCE). There are various references to malaria-like diseases in the medical texts of many ancient civilizations. Apparently Babylonians, Egyptians, Indians, and Chinese all suffered from fatal fevers. Since it was generally believed that some angry god caused malaria, the most popular cures included amulets and lucky charms, magic rituals, sacrifices, and special potions made from medicinal herbs.

By 1000 BCE, outbreaks of malaria were already common in Mediterranean countries such as Greece. In fact, the Greek word for fever was almost always associated with malaria. In his influential writings, the famous Greek doctor Hippocrates (460–377 BCE) was the first to identify the cycles of malarial fevers, as well as the disease's link to the stagnant waters of swamps and

Hippocrates, known as the Father of Medicine, made hypotheses about the origins of malaria.

Malaria

marshes. In fact, Hippocrates believed that warm and humid weather in itself was very unhealthy. He held the weather directly responsible for many ailments, including malaria.

Some historians believe that malaria was partially to blame for the decline of Ancient Greece. They claim that the disease, responsible not only for many deaths but also for the many citizens whose slow recoveries left them incapacitated, led to a weakened society. This in turn made it difficult to govern the country, since rulers kept perishing; to defend it with fewer soldiers; and even to eat, since many farms were abandoned.

Centuries later, when the Roman Empire fell into serious decline, malaria was once again a major factor. Although malaria had been around Ancient Rome for centuries, up until around 400 BCE it appeared in only a mild form. However, changes in climate and the cutting down of forests for farmland, which, when abandoned, led to the formation of marshes, made the area much more inviting for tougher mosquitoes, the real culprits, to carry stronger strains of malaria from Africa. The result was a series of major epidemics over a period of decades, which devastated Roman society.

During the centuries that followed, known as the Dark Ages, much of the medical knowledge the Greeks and Romans had gained about malaria was forgotten. Malaria itself lost its identity and became confused with other types of feverish illnesses. In the meantime,

Famous Faces of Malaria

Malaria has been around since before humans existed. Perhaps it even infected the first animals on Earth. Many famous people, from early history to the present day, have suffered from malaria, including:

- Genghis Khan
- Oliver Cromwell
- Lord Byron
- George Washington

- Abraham Lincoln
- John F. Kennedy
- Mother Theresa
- George Clooney

Some lived, some died, but all of these notable figures knew firsthand the devastating effects of this disease.

as sanitation methods used by the Greeks and Romans were neglected, the disease continued to spread through Europe. By the sixth century, people were coming down with malaria in England, France, Holland, and even as far north as Scandinavia.

At this point, malaria was blamed on angry gods bent on punishing humans, as well as on supposedly weird alignments of certain heavenly stars and planets. It was thought that to cure malaria, you had to get rid of the bad "humors," which were bodily fluids associated with certain moods and illnesses, that could poison your body if you had too many. You could do this by bleeding, or making cuts in your skin that would allow bad fluids to escape; by purging, which you did by drinking herbal potions that would cause you to vomit the so-called poisons out of your system; or cauterization, which involved branding your skin with a hot iron. By the twelfth century, malaria was common all over Europe.

When the first Spanish conquistadors arrived in the New World, hot on the heels of Christopher Columbus, the disease tagged along with them and spread throughout the Americas. In fact, the business of "discovering" and colonizing the world made it very easy for new strains of malaria to spread all over the globe, courtesy of European adventurers and their ships.

Malaria spread throughout Europe for several centuries, starting in the 1500s. The disease was **endemic** to the continent, meaning that is was so common and prevalent in the region that it was a characteristic of the region. While the threat of malaria was constant, there were still epidemic spikes of the disease. One such outbreak occurred in Italy in 1602, killing more than 40,000. It was not until later, however, that the disease extended to other parts of the world.

Malaria Goes Global

two

The original inhabitants of the New World did have to deal with pesky mosquitoes, but it doesn't appear that the locals had to contend with malaria. This was in part because the particular parasite carrying the disease was not native to that part of the world. However, that all changed when the Spanish crossed the Atlantic and conquered the Mayan and Aztec communities living there.

Malaria is transferred from parasite to mosquito to human, and cannot be caught from humans interacting with each other. However, along with multiple diseases unknown to the locals of South and Central America, the Spanish also brought people already infected with malaria. As the American mosquitoes bit infected victims, they pulled the parasites inside their bodies. When they next bit an unaffected, indigenous human, these mosquitoes infected them—changing their lives, and the history of disease in that part of the world, forever.

Prior to the arrival of Europeans, Native people died from diseases but not to the extent that they did once Europeans appeared.

An Old Disease Comes to the New World

Before the arrival of Europeans, the Native people of the Americas dealt with their share of wars, illnesses, and hardships. They had established thriving civilizations in jungle and forest growth, and had their own languages, beliefs, and medical practices. Despite this, the Europeans who arrived on these continents considered the Native communities to be less sophisticated than their own. While some Native groups, such as the Aztecs, welcomed the newcomers, the Europeans wanted to control the land and cared little for the people they met. Soon, settlers became greedy and enslaved or killed the people who helped them, taking over the land for themselves. While for the most part the illnesses they brought devastated these thriving communities unexpectedly, in some instances, such as in the case of Lord Jeffery Amherst and his troops, some European conquerors deliberately infected the Native people with diseases, a type of early biological warfare. In any event, millions of men, women, and children perished from the many deadly European diseases ravaging their population.

As the Native people of North and South America kept dying, European settlers started importing boatloads of slaves from Africa to work their vast sugarcane, tobacco, and cotton plantations. If Africans seemed sturdier and less vulnerable to malaria than

Native Americans, it was undoubtedly because malaria originated in Africa in the first place. Over the centuries, this had allowed Africans' immune systems to build up a natural resistance to the disease. Of course, when these enslaved people were transported across the ocean, they also brought malaria along with them.

Thanks to these early European settlers, malaria was already a fact of life when the original thirteen colonies of the United States were founded. In fact, it was present during numerous important occasions in American history. The disease quite literally played a part in American independence: One of the first military expenditures passed by Congress in 1775 was for $300 to buy quinine, a type of "cure" made from the bark of a cinchona tree, to protect General Washington's troops.

Later, during the Civil War (1861–1865), between 50 and 80 percent of the soldiers in the Union army came down with the disease each year. Prominent U.S. politicians, such as Abraham Lincoln and Ulysses S. Grant, suffered from the disease. In fact, for a long time, malaria was endemic in areas such as the Mississippi Valley and around the Chesapeake Bay.

Even chilly Canada was not safe from malaria. In the summer of 1828, "swamp fever" broke out in the village of Bytown, which later became the Canadian capital of Ottawa. It is believed to have been brought over by infected British soldiers who had been in the

The Power of Quinine

Long before the first Spanish conquistadors landed in South America, the Native people of Peru and Ecuador had already discovered a potent remedy against bad fevers. Quinine was made by drying and crushing the bark of the cinchona tree. Named after the countess of Chinchón, wife of the viceroy of Peru, the tree is found in tropical areas of South America, and was thought to be a cure for malaria. Upon taking the crushed bark, people's symptoms remarkably improved. The need for this "miracle cure" was great in Europe, and when it first arrived in the 1700s, having been brought over by Jesuit missionaries, people clamored for the drug.

Quinine was especially popular with Europe's royal families. Since so many kings and queens had died of malaria, many royals reached for quinine the minute their foreheads felt warm. In malaria-infested India, quinine became the rage as well, although in another form. Since tonic water contained quinine, the refreshing combination of gin and tonic became a classic antimalarial cocktail among British colonial rulers.

While this remedy seemed promising, it did not completely cure the suffering individual. It was later discovered to weaken

The cinchona tree.

the parasite that produces malaria, although it did not completely kill it. Therefore, as long as the person kept taking quinine, symptoms seemed to improve. Once they stopped, however, they could suffer from another attack of malaria, called a relapse. Taking quinine could also have long-lasting **side effects**, such as deafness, distortion to vision, and stomach problems. However, the Centers for Disease Control and Prevention (CDC) still recommends using quinine in some instances to battle the disease.

British colony of India. By the time the Canadian cold had killed off the mosquitoes in September, many people had already succumbed to what had quickly become an epidemic.

Several major medical breakthroughs in understanding what caused malaria occurred in the late 1800s. It was widely understood at that time that microscopic organisms, other than bacteria and viruses, were responsible for causing many diseases. Louis Pasteur had first tested this "germ theory" in the 1860s. It was clear something other than a virus or bacteria was at work in transmitting malaria, and the medical community wanted to know what.

In 1880, a French army surgeon named Alphonse Laveran (1845–1922) had been working in Algeria, where he had studied closely patients who had died from malaria, then called marsh fever.

Alphonse Laveran was the first person to observe the malaria parasite.

At that time, malaria was a very serious illness affecting many members of the army. Laveran was determined to find out what truly caused malaria. On November 6, 1880, he made an exciting discovery: elements moving on the edges of sphere-shaped bodies in red blood cells. This was part of the life cycle of the parasite that causes malaria, and it signaled the first time a parasite had been viewed in connection with the disease. This was a massive advancement for human understanding of malaria. He published his findings, titled *Treatise on Marsh Fevers*, in 1884, informing the rest of the world and completing a vital piece of the malaria puzzle. For his efforts, Laveran received a Nobel Prize in 1907.

Ten years later, another medical advancement for malaria occurred. Surgeon Ronald Ross (1857–1932) became intent on solving the mystery of malaria when he was stationed in malaria-infested India. During a trip to London in 1894, Ross looked up a colleague named Patrick Manson. While working in China, Manson had discovered that when mosquitoes fed on blood from animals, they also sucked up parasites before passing them along to their next meal. Could this be the key to the spread of malaria? Intrigued by the possibility, Ross returned to India determined to test out this idea.

We know now that mosquitoes pass the parasite on to human or animal **hosts**. When a mosquito bites an infected human or animal, it also sucks up the parasite lurking in the human's bloodstream. When this same

Early Remedies
for Malaria

As humans' understanding of illnesses advanced, there were a number of other contributors thought to cause malaria. One supposed source was the effect of the sun's heat on stagnant water. The resulting evaporation was thought to release poisonous vapors into the air—this is perhaps one explanation of why malaria was named *mal'aria*, meaning "bad air." As a "cure," lightning from frequent storms was thought to zap the deadly vapors away. Other supposed malaria sources ranged from overeating to undercooking meat, drinking well water, and sucking oranges at night.

Many elements were thought to bring about the disease and its consequences, so when quinine was first introduced, people thought it was truly miraculous. It could take away symptoms of the disease relatively painlessly. However, other curing methods were not as pleasant as quinine. In 1833, the sister of Emperor Pedro II of Brazil, Princess Paula Mariana, came down with a bad case of malaria. The royal doctors not only made her take quinine both orally and anally, they also stuffed her with soups and applied bloodsucking leeches, mustard plaster, and burning chemicals to her skin. It was a very painful process, and sadly the girl passed away just before her tenth birthday.

Stories such as these were common throughout the eighteenth and nineteenth centuries, and contributed to the rising death toll of people infected with malaria. However, as medical advancements were made throughout the decades, it became apparent that there were more effective, and certain, ways of combatting and even preventing malaria throughout the world.

mosquito bites its next victim, it releases the parasite into their bloodstream and infects them. Thus, a cycle of infection begins. In the late 1800s, little was known about this method of transmission, but Ross suspected he'd found something promising.

After two years of experiments, on August 20, 1897 (which he later called "Mosquito Day"), Ross found a human malaria parasite in the stomach of a mosquito that had fed on a malaria patient. He was so excited by his discovery that he wrote a poem predicting mosquitoes' eventual day of reckoning.

Unfortunately, Ross was unable to prove the entire sequence of infection using human guinea pigs. In 1898, he was able to show how a mosquito that had fed on a bird with malaria then bit a healthy bird and infected it. However, at this time in Rome, the Italian zoologist Giovanni Batista Grassi beat him to the punch. Carrying out the same experiment with mosquitoes and humans, Grassi succeeded in confirming how human malaria was spread.

In spite of this setback, Ross dedicated the rest of his life to finding ways of preventing the spread of the disease. His efforts were rewarded when he won a Nobel Prize for medicine in 1902.

After these discoveries, people became more knowledgeable about the cause of malaria, and many researchers throughout the world tried to come up with a definite cure. For the most part, they used quinine and other already existing remedies. However, modern advancements, particularly in the dye industry, spurred on the discovery of new methods of treatment. The first instance of this happened in 1891, when a German microbiologist named Paul Ehrlich used a dye called methylene blue to better view malaria parasites under a microscope. As the parasite came into contact with the dye, it took it in at a fast pace. This behavior indicated to Ehrlich that perhaps the dye killed the parasite. He attempted to find out by treating two malaria patients with the dye. The disease seemed to leave them, and thus another "cure" was born. In the years following, many others produced other possible remedies, and made several attempts at vaccines, but no methods were 100 percent effective.

In the United States, outbreaks of malaria continued well into the 1940s. In 1914 alone, there were more than 600,000 cases of malaria recorded in the United States. Although today it is quite rare, there are nonetheless close to 1,500 Americans who are infected with malaria each year, most while traveling abroad. The disease hit a forty-year high in 2011 with 1,925 cases according to the Centers for Disease Control and Prevention. Since the outbreaks were limited, mosquito-control efforts were not needed. However, since malaria-carrying mosquitoes tend to spend their summers "vacationing" throughout most of the United States, the possibility of the disease reestablishing itself is a possibility.

Malaria in the Modern World

After years of decline, cases of malaria increased through the beginning of the twenty-first century. While much more media attention is given to AIDS and the Ebola virus, malaria still wipes out millions every year. It is a public health problem in some ninety-seven countries worldwide. This puts billions of people at risk, roughly around 36 percent of the world's population, in fact. According to estimates made by the World Health Organization (WHO), malaria infects about 200 million people each year. Of these victims, 91 percent live in Africa.

With its hot climate and muggy rainy conditions, sub-Saharan Africa is a breeding ground for mosquitoes carrying the malaria parasite. Experts estimate that an average person in Africa receives as many as 120 infective mosquito bites each year. While there is some resistance to the disease based on its prevalence in the area, millions of Africans continue to die every day. Many victims are infants and children living in rural areas without access to efficient health care. In fact, it is estimated that a child dies every minute from malaria in Africa. According to the international advocacy organization ONE, each year $12 billion is lost from the African economy due to malaria. Methods of containing the disease have been introduced and used in many areas of the country for decades, and

Africa has the most cases of malaria reported each year.

while cases are decreasing, malaria is still a grave illness devastating that part of the world. However, Africa is not alone. Other regions of Asia and Latin America also continue to suffer from the disease. The WHO has made malaria control a top global priority, and efforts to tame, treat, and eliminate the disease continue every day.

three The Malaria Cycle

Malaria is able to spread through a cycle involving the parasite that causes the disease, the mosquitoes that spread the parasite, and the humans that suffer from the disease and also help to spread the parasite. Although malaria has been around for centuries, scientists only began to understand fully how the disease spread in the latter half of the nineteenth century onward.

Key Players in Malaria Advancement

Several people were crucial to furthering our knowledge of malaria. These included Alphonse Laveran and Ronald Ross, as well as Italians Giovanni Batista Grassi and Raimondo Filetti, who were behind naming two of the five different malaria parasites that infect humans. The man responsible for naming the most deadly parasite, *Plasmodium*

An artistic representation of the malaria parasite in red blood cells.

falciparum, was American William H. Welch, who discovered it in 1897. While it became clear in the 1880s that a parasite was responsible for causing the disease, it was unknown exactly how the parasite entered a human's body and what happened afterward.

The Anopheles Mosquito

The big answer to just how the parasite infected humans turned out to be via mosquitoes. For quite some time, mosquitoes had been suspects: As early as 1717, an Italian doctor named Giovanni Maria Lancisi suggested mosquitoes' involvement in the spread of malaria. However, they weren't proven guilty until much later. In fact, it was not until 1897 that the riddle was officially solved by Ronald Ross.

As both Ross and Giovanni Batista Grassi discovered, not just any old mosquito can be a carrier of human malaria. The culprit was proven to be a striped-winged mosquito belonging to the Anopheles genus, or family. Female Anopheles need human blood to provide energy for the eggs they lay. Because of this, when evening comes around, their favorite feeding time, the ladies go hunting. Not only can they see you and smell you from up to sixty feet (18.3 m) away, but they can also detect the radiation given off by your warm body. Once they have tracked you down, the hungry females get to work sucking blood from their human host. If the host in question happens to be infected with a malaria parasite, this gets sucked up as well.

The Five *Plasmodium* Parasites

In nature, a parasite is a creature or organism that lives on or inside another creature. The malaria parasite is a tiny thing that goes by the name of *plasmodium*. Although almost all mammals can be infected by *plasmodium* parasites, in most cases, different animal species can be infected only by their own particular species of the parasite. Humans, for example, usually can't get malaria from the same kind of parasites that infect monkeys, birds, or snakes. To date, there are five species of malaria parasites that are known to make people sick: *Plasmodium falciparum*, *Plasmodium vivax*, *Plasmodium ovale*, *Plasmodium malariae*, and *Plasmodium knowlesi*. The most deadly of all is *Plasmodium falciparum*, which can cause such lethal complications as malaria of the brain.

While the first sighting of a malaria parasite was made in 1880 by Alphonse Laveran, initially the medical community rejected his discovery. It was only in 1886 that Italian scientists (due to the many malaria epidemics in Italy, Italians were the leading specialists) officially recognized the parasite as the source of the disease.

The female Anopheles mosquito is responsible for transmitting the malaria parasite to humans and animals.

Inside the mosquito, the parasite spends two to three weeks going through a period of complex changes. During this time it becomes infectious. It then moves up to the mosquito's saliva glands, where it lies, ready and waiting, for the bug to bite its next human victim.

When you are bitten by an infected Anopheles mosquito, the parasite then moves in and infects you. Once inside of you, the threadlike parasite enters your bloodstream and is carried to your liver, where it begins reproducing aggressively. New offspring are then rereleased into the bloodstream where they attack and destroy the red blood cells, which carry oxygen

Bite-Sized Facts About Mosquitoes

- There are more than 3,000 different species of these pesky bugs.

- The average mosquito weighs 2 to 2.5 milligrams.

- Male mosquitoes don't suck blood, only females do it (an average drink is five-millionths of a liter).

- If the sensory nerve in a mosquito's stomach is cut, it will keep sucking blood until it bursts.

- Mosquitoes whiz around at the speed of around 1 mile (1.6 kilometers) per hour.

- Although some mosquitoes can travel distances of up to 100 miles (161 km), most fly within a radius of only one mile (1.6 km) throughout their entire lifetimes.

- In warm weather, mosquitoes can produce a new generation in a mere week.

throughout your body. From time to time, a new form of the parasite bursts forth from the destroyed blood cells and travels through your bloodstream, invading new blood cells. Such bursts are responsible for the peaks of malarial fever that victims experience. The five different malaria parasites produce different fever cycles in which a fever rises, falls, and rises again. *Plasmodium falciparum*, for example, has a forty-eight-hour period between fever peaks. In a malaria patient, these cycles of attacks and fevers continue over and over until natural or acquired immunity, antimalarial remedies, or death bring the repetitive process to an end.

Worldwide Travelers

Although Anopheles rarely fly more than a couple of miles from their homes, they have been known to hitch rides on airplanes and high-speed ships. In 1928, a French ship carrying mail from western Africa to northern Brazil also carried along an African variety of Anopheles that until then had been unknown in South America. The imported mosquito turned out to be much more efficient at spreading malaria than its Brazilian cousin. In no time, Brazil was in the throes of the worst epidemic it had ever experienced. Deaths were so plentiful that entire districts were wiped out.

Because of such "accidents," international law requires disinsectization of all aircrafts and ships prior to their departure, and enforces rigid anti-mosquito sanitation in all ports and airports.

Malaria lurks in mosquitoes living in tropical climates.
Take precautions when traveling.

Although Anopheles inhabit tropical regions, neither the mosquitoes nor their parasitic guests can survive cold temperatures. Anything below 15 degrees Celsius, or 59 degrees Fahrenheit, is fatal to both. Very few malarial Anopheles hang out in tropical forests. This is because female mosquitoes lay their eggs to hatch in small, sunlit areas of water. Dense tropical jungles tend to be pretty dark. Mosquitoes appreciate it when humans come along and, for whatever reason, clear farmland or cut down forests. The treeless land provides mosquitoes with both the ideal conditions and the proximity to human hosts that they require to reproduce. Since, from the beginning of civilization, humans have been quite happy to cut down forests, both mosquitoes and malaria have thrived over the centuries. More recently, irrigation projects, dams, and improper sewage systems in overcrowded city slums have done much to increase the explosion of "man-made" malaria.

Spreading Malaria Across the Globe

As we have seen, human beings are the source of the malaria parasites that infect other humans. Malaria-bearing mosquitoes don't stray far from home. However, the same cannot be said of malaria-carrying humans. Over time, invading armies, explorers and traders, colonists and settlers, immigrants and refugees all played their parts in spreading malaria around the world. During World War II alone, more than 500,000 American soldiers were interned for malaria caught overseas. Today, with increased travel to far-flung destinations, many North American tourists have returned to their malaria-free hometowns from a trip to the tropics, carrying the parasite with them.

In Africa, where the situation is extreme, there are many regions in which malaria is endemic. As a result of being bitten and rebitten, infected and reinfected throughout their lives, many Africans build up immunity to the disease. This means that although the *plasmodium* parasites might live within them throughout their lives, they will either suffer from mild symptoms from time to time or not experience any symptoms at all. In such endemic areas, children are protected in their first months of life by the disease-fighting **antibodies** produced by their immune mothers. After that, if they don't die from the disease (and, tragically, many do), they develop their own immunity over the years.

This developed immunity is not a permanent shield against malaria. If an immune adult leaves an area that is rife with malaria, they will start to lose their immunity, and will find themselves capable of getting the disease about one or two years later. Even more concerning is that these adults are carriers of the disease, meaning they could cause an outbreak of malaria wherever they travel, even if they don't show any signs of having the disease. This is one of the ways that new outbreaks can flare up in areas that previously seemed to be free from malaria. Immigrants and folks traveling around the world continue the global spread of malaria.

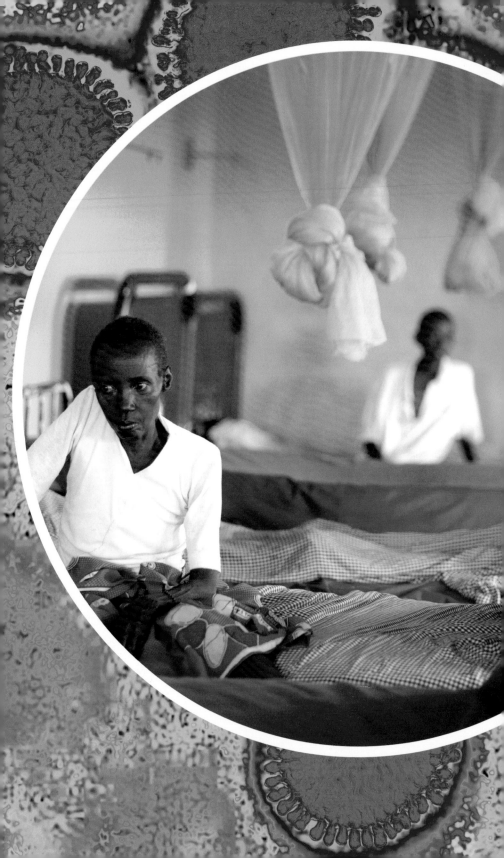

four Understanding, Treating, and Preventing Malaria

T hankfully, medical research has advanced in modern times to allow for malaria to be curbed in many parts of the world. The development of antimalarial drugs has helped keep cases of malaria in people who travel abroad to relatively low numbers. However, instances of the disease continue to occur every day. When traveling to another country, it is best to do all that you can to prevent yourself from acquiring the disease.

Contracting Malaria

Once you are bitten by an infected Anopheles mosquito, the plasmodium parasite will take a while to make its effects known. Depending on the *plasmodium* in question, this can range from nine days (*Plasmodium falciparum*) to thirty days (*Plasmodium malariae*). Some strains of *Plasmodium vivax* might take up to nine months before they start doing their dirty work.

This patient waits in a severe malaria ward in Rwanda.

The first sign you might have malaria is if you suddenly break out in a fever. At first this might seem to be the flu. However, if you have the slightest doubt, check it out. Most deaths are due to uncomplicated attacks of *Plasmodium falciparum* that, left unchecked, lead to severe cases.

Aside from fevers that come and go, other signs of malaria include headaches, aches and pains all over, diarrhea, shaking chills, sweating, and abdominal pains. If left untreated, malaria will leave you weak, groggy, and with yellowish skin. As the parasites increasingly clog your bloodstream, the disease can lead to vomiting and convulsions, and, finally, kidney failure and/or cerebral malaria, in which victims fall into a coma and never awaken. Needless to say, both of these extreme conditions spell death.

Meanwhile, it is still uncertain whether the parasites cause mosquitoes as much harm as they do humans. It is generally believed that malaria-carrying mosquitoes do live shorter lives than their non-infected winged counterparts.

Avoiding Malaria

If malaria comes from parasites living in mosquitoes, how do you avoid catching it? There are several ways you can try to prevent the disease, including:

- Stay away from risky, endemic regions (check with the CDC: www.cdc.gov).

Bed nets are important to have when in malaria-affected regions of the world.

- Try to travel after peak mosquito season (when it's cold).

- When mosquitoes are outside (generally at dusk and dawn), stay inside.

- Make sure your living quarters have screens on the windows and doors.

- If necessary, sleep under a mosquito net (without holes, and if possible, soaked in insecticide).

- Use mosquito repellents such as DEET.

- Soak your clothing in an insecticide called permethrin. One treatment will stay on through several washings.

- Wear long-sleeved clothing and long pants. Avoid dark colors, which mosquitoes love.

- Put up either a bat house or a house for purple martins. Both of these winged creatures love mosquitoes and eat hundreds every hour.

Halting Malaria

Over the years, many different techniques have been used to try to stop malaria. One of the most promising was invented in the 1940s. Dichloro-diphenyl-trichloroethane (DDT), a type of insecticide, effectively killed malaria-carrying mosquitoes. It was the most widely used insect-killing tool for decades and continues to be used in some parts of the world today. However, DDT was also found to cause harm to the environment, and it was eventually prohibited in the United States. While other countries still decide whether to use DDT to spray inside homes in regions where malaria-carrying mosquitoes and other insects are prevalent, more and more mosquitoes and other pests are becoming resistant to the spray, and other methods for protection are needed.

Another way of combating the disease also formed in the 1940s, when scientists began to **synthesize**, or make in a laboratory from chemicals, different natural

Why We're Still Struggling Against Malaria

- Even as scientists began discovering the poisonous effect of DDT on friendly birds and bugs, not to mention humans who ate DDT-sprayed fruits, rougher and tougher Anopheles mosquitoes had already built up resistance to the toxic spray.

- Malaria parasites became resistant to chloroquine and then to other, newer antimalarials such as mefloquine.

- Increased travel and international trade sent drug-resistant parasites all over the globe.

- Tougher and more widespread efforts to fight malaria grew more and more expensive. Many governments in poorer countries of Africa, Latin America, and Southeast Asia couldn't afford to pay for the health, education, and agricultural programs needed to control the disease.

drugs to fight off malaria, such as quinine, chloroquine, doxycycline, mefloquine (larium), and artemisinin. Your doctor usually prescribes these drugs before you go on vacation to a place where malaria is common. The kind of antimalarial your doctor recommends depends on any medical conditions you might have and where you are traveling. All of these antimalarials are preventive medications. They do not guarantee 100 percent protection. In fact, today, many Anopheles mosquitoes in some parts of the world are becoming resistant to these antimalarial drugs. The need for another type of prevention method is becoming increasingly crucial.

It may not be long before this need is fulfilled. The search for an effective vaccine continues, but recent developments seem promising. In 2009, pharmaceutical company GlaxoSmithKline (GSK) developed a new vaccine called RTS,S that is producing surprising results—in children aged 5 months to 17 months, instances of the disease were almost halved. As of 2014, RTS,S was in a third stage of human trials. However, rival company Sanaria also has a successful vaccine, called PfSPZ, which is perhaps even more effective than RTS,S. Sanaria's early clinical trials found PfSPZ eliminated malaria in 100 percent of cases that received the highest dose. It is suspected that GSK's vaccine could be available as early as 2015, and Sanaria's by 2017. While the race continues, the best way to treat malaria is not to get it, or let it (or rather the mosquitoes that carry it) get you.

Determining If You Have Malaria

Diagnosing malaria properly and quickly is key to staying alive. If you have been in an area with malaria and if, even a year later, you are experiencing any of the symptoms previously mentioned, see a doctor immediately. Because early flulike symptoms can resemble one of many other diseases, including typhoid and meningitis, your doctor will need to take a blood sample. If you do have malaria, the parasites will show up—if not right away, then soon enough—under the microscope, swimming around in your red blood cells.

Treatment Options

If you've been diagnosed with malaria, a doctor will probably set a course of treatment that is driven by how severe your case is. Where you got the malaria, and the specific parasite that infected you, is also part of the equation, particularly if the strain of malaria you have is resistant to common antimalarial drugs. Often, the first stage of treatment involves intravenous drugs using a needle to place the drugs directly in your blood, but with time, you can start taking the medicine orally. The medical staff will keep a close eye on you, as they need to ensure you don't suffer any side effects from the drugs. The cure should not be worse than the disease.

Continuing the Fight Against Malaria

five

S ince the culprits responsible for malaria were first identified in the late 1800s, people around the world have made an effort to conquer the parasite and mosquito pair. In the aftermath of World War II, the world united on a global front against malaria as a common enemy, and it was a war we seemed to be slowly winning. This effort to eliminate a disease from the planet was suggested by the World Health Organization in 1955 and known as the Global Malaria Eradication campaign. The health agency recommended combatting malaria by spraying insecticide in regions where malaria was dominant. Around the world, people sprayed the usual places mosquitoes lurked—houses, fields, and swamps—with DDT. They coated marshes with paraffin (a waxy substance used for sealing and coating that also prevents mosquito larvae from breathing) and drained stagnant, or standing, water. These measures, along with the

People around the world try to combat malaria by spraying insecticides such as DDT.

widespread use of the antimalarial chloroquine, had impressive results. Malaria was completely eliminated from countries such as Italy, Spain, Hungary, Portugal, and the United States. While in others, at least until the end of the 1960s, malaria was definitely retreating.

However, in many tropical nations, Mother Nature's perverse ways, coupled with environmental disturbances and reduced government budgets, combined forces to put an end to the WHO's plan to completely **eradicate** malaria once and for all in 1972.

Today, people around the world are again united in an effort to combat the spread of malaria. Agencies such as the WHO and CDC host websites featuring detailed information about the disease, and every year on April 25 the world observes World Malaria Day, a time to learn about malaria and ways to prevent it. Likewise, while the possibility of completely eliminating the disease from the world is not likely to be achieved soon, various researchers are doing all they can to invent new and innovative ways of controlling and halting the disease at every step of its existence.

Taking Malaria Out of the Mosquitoes

In addition to developing new malaria vaccines, scientists looking to wipe out malaria have recently been testing two new methods to combat the disease. In 2014, researchers suggested using genetic

Scientists are inventing new ways to modify mosquitoes to resist the malaria parasite.

engineering on mosquitoes to make them resistant to the parasite that ultimately causes malaria. The technology, called Crispr, is still being tested, but it allows scientists to make targeted and specific changes to a mosquito's DNA. Scientists would use it to create insects immune to the malaria parasite. These bugs would then mate with other mosquitoes and pass the immunity to future generations.

There's still much to decide about this process specifically, and genetic engineering in general. Some people question whether making these changes is ethical, while others are concerned that the tampering could result in more dangerous consequences down the road, with crossbreeding and mutations creating more deadly breeds. These broader possibilities must be weighed against the possibility of slowing down or even halting such a deadly disease.

Another development in the fight against malaria comes from Sanaria, the American company trying to create an effective malaria vaccine. According to *The New York Times*, the company also wants to enlist robots to "do what now requires a line of trained humans with microscopes: dissecting half-frozen mosquitoes with tiny needles to extract their salivary glands." These glands are where the malaria parasite is injected into a human. By removing the parasite after dousing it in radiation and inserting it into humans, it is thought the human will develop a sense of immunity to the disease, much like vaccine in a shot.

Nothing but Nets

One of the most used treatments against malaria over the decades has been bed nets. If these thick nets are dipped in insecticide, it is thought that they will keep out the malaria-carrying mosquito. However, studies of people given these bed nets show that they are not always effective. As mentioned earlier, many mosquitoes are developing resistance to insecticides. People living in endemic areas likewise don't always

Giving Cows a New Smell

As researchers look to end malaria, they are willing to use any and all methods to stop the disease and save lives. Mosquitoes target humans for biting because of the unique aroma humans have. One unique plan to confuse the mosquitoes involves creating a perfume that would mimic a human smell and spray cows with the scent. The company developing the idea, ISCA Technologies, hopes that the mosquitoes would then bite the cows instead of people.

Don't worry about the cows. They will not contract malaria from the bites, but they might just save some human lives.

You can only prevent malaria by taking the right steps to protect yourself and your family.

know how to use the nets. According to the British newspaper *The Guardian*, some people use the nets for other things: "fishing, for use as sieves or even for wedding dress material." While these other uses may seem strange to you, there is an explanation why people choose to do this. In these areas, people are susceptible to malaria, but some tend to view the disease as a rite of passage, similar to how chicken pox is viewed in the United States. In several instances of the lighter forms of malaria, the disease goes away on its own. Quite a few people, unaware that mosquitoes carry malaria, also associate the disease with getting too much sun, eating too many peanuts, or using too much red palm oil.

The bed nets themselves have flaws. They are stiflingly hot to sleep under, for one. Also, they do not last forever. It is estimated that bed nets expire and need replacing after three years. Moreover, it's unsure how effective the nets are in keeping out mosquitoes. People who used mosquito nets were not always protected from acquiring the disease. Still, these techniques are used throughout the world and have proven to curb, in some part, the spread of malaria.

Educating people is key to tackling the spread of malaria. With the work of agencies such as the Malaria Vaccine Initiative, world medical organizations, and the numerous charities bringing nets to Africa and other developing nations, the hope is to either eliminate or significantly reduce the number of people who suffer from malaria worldwide. The challenge remains great, but just as science has won its wars against other diseases such as smallpox, the world hopes that malaria can eventually become a deadly footnote in history.

Glossary

antibodies Proteins produced by your immune system that attack foreign viruses and bacteria.

antimalarial Medicine used to fight the malaria parasite.

diagnosis Identification of a disease based on signs and symptoms.

endemic Native to a particular people or country.

epidemic When an infectious disease spreads beyond a local population and infects many more people throughout a region.

eradicate To get rid of completely.

host Plant or animal that provides housing and food for a parasite.

immunity Ability to resist a particular disease.

pandemic Uncontrolled outbreak of an infectious disease on a global scale.

parasite Creature or organism that lives on or inside another creature.

quinine First cure for malaria; made from the dried crushed bark of the cinchona tree.

side effects Secondary or adverse reactions to taking drugs or medications.

symptoms Signs or characteristics of a disease that can be felt (fever, chills, swelling) by a patient.

synthesize To produce a substance by combining different chemical elements.

For More Information

Interested in learning more about malaria? Check out these websites and organizations.

Websites

Cool Facts and Tips About Malaria

www.eschooltoday.com/malaria/malaria-facts-and-tips-for-kids.html

This interactive website for kids gives you the most important facts and tips about malaria.

KidsHealth: Malaria

kidshealth.org/parent/infections/parasitic/malaria.html

This website details information about malaria, how it is spread, and ways of preventing it.

National Geographic: Malaria

video.nationalgeographic.com/video/malaria-sci

This video illustrates the seriousness of malaria and how it is being treated in Central Africa.

Nothing but Nets

nothingbutnets.net

This website discusses Nothing but Nets, a charitable organization looking to raise funds to provide life-saving mosquito nets to people in need of them.

PATH Malaria Vaccine Initiative

www.malariavaccine.org

This official website for this charitable organization updates new research and partnerships.

Organizations

Centers for Disease Control and Prevention (CDC)
1600 Clifton Road
Atlanta, GA 30333
Website: www.cdc.gov

The Pan American Health Organization
Regional Office of the World Health Organization
525 Twenty-third Street NW
Washington, DC 20037
Website: www.paho.org

For Further Reading

Bungay Stainer, Michael. *End Malaria*. Seattle, WA:
The Domino Project, 2011.

Masterson, Karen M. *The Malaria Project: The U.S.
Government's Secret Mission to Find a Miracle Cure*.
New York, NY: Penguin Group, 2014.

Packard, Randall M. *The Making of a Tropical Disease:
A Short History of Malaria*. Baltimore, MD:
Johns Hopkins University Press, 2014.

Shah, Sonia. *The Fever: How Malaria Has Ruled
Humankind for 500,000 Years*. New York, NY:
Sarah Crichton Books, 2010.

Webb, James L. A. Jr. *Humanity's Burden: A Global
History of Malaria*. Studies in Environment and
History. New York, NY: Cambridge University Press,
2008.

Index

acquired immune
   deficiency syndrome
   (AIDS), 11, 30
Africa, 5–6, 12, 15,
   20–21, 30–31, **31**,
   38, 41, 47, 57
antibodies, 41
antimalarial, 12, 22, 38,
   43, 47–49, 52
Asia, 6, 12, 31, 47

bed nets, **45**, 54, 57

Centers for Disease
   Control (CDC), 23,
   44, 52
climate, 15, 30, **39**

Decade to Roll Back
   Malaria, 6, 13
diagnosis, 5, 49
diarrhea, 5, 44

Ebola, 30
endemic, 17, 21, 41, 44, 54

epidemic, 9–11, 15, 17,
   24, 35, 38
eradicate, 52
Europe, 11–12, 16–17, 22

germ theory, 24

host, 25, 34, 40
humors, 17

immunity, 9, 38, 41,
   53–54
India, 22, 24–25
insecticide, 45–46, **51**,
   51, 54
Italy, 17, 35, 52

Latin America, 10,
   31, 47
Laveran, Alphonse, 12,
   24–25, **24**, 33, 35
London, 25

malaria
   avoiding, 44–46

Index

contracting, 7, 7,
43–44, 55
diagnosing, 49
history of, 11–16
man-made, 40
halting the spread of,
46–48
research on, 6, 43
signs of, 41, 44
treatment of, 49
miracle cure, 22
mosquito, 6, 12, 15,
19, 24–25, 28,
30, 33, 37–40, **39**,
44–46, 51–55,
53, 57
Anopheles mosquito,
34, 36, **36**, 43,
47–48
control, 29, 45
Mosquito Day, 28

pandemic, 9, 10
parasite, 6, 12–13, 19,
23, 24, 25, 28– 30,

33–36, **33**, **36**, 38,
40–41, 43–44, 47,
49, 51, 53–54, **53**
Pasteur, Louis, 24
plasmodium, 12–13, 33,
38, 41
parasites, 35, 43–44

quinine, 12, 21–23, 26,
28, 48

Ross, Ronald, 12, 25,
28, 33–34

side effects, 23, 49
Spanish flu, 9
swamp fever, 21
symptoms, 5, 22–23, 26,
41, 49
synthesize, 46

Welch, William H., 34
World Health Organization
(WHO), 13, 30, 31, 52